GARDEN DESIGN

p

GARDEN DESIGN

KATHARINA TURNER

Illustrations by
FENJA GUNN

This is a Parragon Book
This edition published in 2004

Parragon
Queen Street House
4 Queen Street
Bath BA1 1HE

Produced by
Robert Ditchfield Ltd

ISBN 1-40540-154-0

A copy of the British Library Cataloguing in Publication Data is
avaliable from the Library.

Printed in China

ACKNOWLEDGEMENTS

The publishers would like to thank the many people and organizations who have allowed photographs to be taken for this book, including the following:

Burford House, Tenbury Wells; Les Dallow; Mr and Mrs K. Dawson, Chennels Gate, Eardisley; Richard Edwards, Well Cottage, Blakemere; Elm Close; Mrs G.A. Follis; Milton Grundy; Mr J. Hargraves; Lance Hattatt, Arrow Cottage, Weobley; Hergest Croft Gardens; Mrs R. Humphries, Orchard Bungalow, Bishops Frome; Mrs David Lewis; Ash Farm, Much Birch; Mr and Mrs R. Norman, Marley Bank, Whitbourne; Polesden Lacy (National Trust); Mary Ann Robinson; Duncan Rogers; Sissinghurst Castle (National Trust); Malcolm Skinner, Eastgrove Cottage Gardens, Shrawley; Mr and Mrs P.J. Strevens; Mr Taylor; Malley Terry, 28 Hillgrove Cresent, Kidderminster; Mr and Mrs R.J. Tingley; Raymond Treasure, Stockton Bury Farm, Kimbolton; Mrs Trevor-Jones, Preen Manor; Mr And Mrs S de R Wall; Mr and Mrs Geoffrey Williams, Close Farm Crockham Hill; Mrs David William-Thomas, The Manor House, Birlingham; York Gate, Leeds.

We would like to thank especially Queenswood Garden Centre, Wellington, Hereford for their help.

CONTENTS

POISONOUS PLANTS

In recent years, concern has been voiced about poisonous plants or plants which can cause allergic reactions if touched. The fact is that many plants are poisonous, some in a particular part, others in all their parts. For the sake of safety, it is always, without exception, essential to assume that no part of a plant should be eaten unless it is known, without any doubt whatsoever, that the plant or its part is edible and that it cannot provoke an allergic reaction in the individual person who samples it. It must also be remembered that some plants can cause severe dermatitis, blistering or an allergic reaction if touched, in some individuals and not in others. It is the responsibility of the individual to take all the above into account.

WATER IN THE GARDEN

All water gardens are beautiful, but sadly they can be dangerous, mostly to children who can drown in even a few inches of water, or sometimes to adults. We would urge readers where necessary to take account of this and provide a reliable means of protection if they include water in the garden.

HOW TO USE THIS BOOK

Where appropriate, approximate measurements of a plant's height have been given, and also the spread where this is significant, in both metric and imperial measures. The height is the first measurement, as for example 1.2m × 60cm/4 × 2ft. However, both height and spread vary so greatly from garden to garden since they depend on soil, climate and position, that these measurements are offered as guides only. This is especially true of trees and shrubs where ultimate growth can be unpredictable.

The following symbols are also used throughout the book:
$\bigcirc$ = thrives best or only in full sun
$\circleurl$ = thrives best or only in part-shade
$\bullet$ = succeeds in full shade
E = evergreen

Where no sun symbol and no reference to sun or shade is made in the text, it can be assumed that the plant tolerates sun or light shade.

PLANT NAMES

For ease of reference this book gives the botanical name under which a plant is most widely listed for the gardener. These names are sometimes changed and in such cases the new name has been included. Common names are given wherever they are in frequent use.

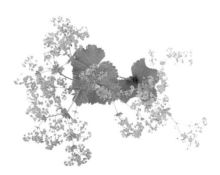

GARDEN DESIGN

THE GARDENS WE REMEMBER with pleasure are the ones which appear to have been set out quite effortlessly. These gardens have style. Yet if we look more closely at them we will find that a considerable amount of thought has gone into the layout. One reason for the success of a garden is when it seems to have become an extension of the house; the terrace for example has been constructed of the same material as the house, or the path which leads into the garden has been centred on the French doors and makes an unbroken transition from house to garden. The colour scheme and shapes of the plants may echo the colour and shapes in the house. The style which emerges is entirely individual to this garden and this is what makes it successful.

How can you make your own garden distinctive? Consider the style of your house and its surroundings. Consider how you and your family will use this outdoor space. Will you sit in it, play in it, entertain in it, grow vegetables and flowers, look at it through the window?

Once you have thought this out, you can really begin to use your imagination; even

A sumptuous garden which completely disguises its boundaries.

9

The flowery profusion of a cottage garden.

The calm control of a Japanese garden.

tiny backyards have been turned into wonderfully exuberant gardens with luscious planting, imaginative paving and judiciously placed statues. Visit gardens, look at books and magazines, take photographs for inspiration. This inspiration and a good understanding of your own site will enable you to find the style suitable for your own garden.

Traditionally gardens are divided into formal and informal gardens. Formal means that the garden is divided by a central axis and often cross axes; beds and borders are surrounded by low hedges. Topiary, ornamental pools, urns, statues and vistas are all parts of a formal garden. Quite often this style is dismissed because of its apparent high cost and maintenance. Yet hedges need to be cut only once or twice a year and the geometric shape of the lawns makes mowing easier.

An informal garden has gentle curves throughout. Beds and borders are part of these gentle curves. Plants spill over onto

A small but charming and restful patio.

Expert use of stone and paving in a small garden.

paths and the atmosphere of the garden is that of vitality. To achieve this gentle rolling style, the design of the curves has to be strong and definite otherwise the garden could look insipid. Large gardens are usually formal near the house and become more informal further away from the house.

It is a good idea to spend some time deciding what type of garden you and your family find most attractive. Is a cottage garden with its emphasis on colourful flower borders what you envisage; or a low-maintenance foliage garden with ferns and ivies, fatsias and oak-leaved hydrangeas; or a magical water garden with formal or wildlife ponds planted with candelabra primulas, irises, rodgersias and gunneras; or a serene oriental garden with its wonderful acers, mosses and symbolic rocks?

Your final decision, of course, will depend on your personal taste and what time and money you are prepared to devote to looking after your garden.

Your Needs and Wants

The idea of listing what you need in your garden is still the most straightforward way and the best way of not forgetting anything. Walk around your garden and make notes. You might like to start at your drive. Do you need additional parking? Is the footpath in the position it is needed or has the postman made his own?

The siting of the bin, wood and coal store, compost heap, garden shed, washing line and greenhouse need to be carefully considered. Does your garden need retaining walls and steps? An irrigation system or at least an outside tap is absolutely essential and should go on your list of needs.

Needs Checklist

Drive	Parking	Washing line
Compost heap	Garden shed	Bonfire area
Greenhouse	Bin area	Vegetable patch
Septic tank	Steps	Retaining wall
Outside tap	Dog kennel	Wood storage
Coal bunker		

An open brick screen will not form a wind tunnel.

Now that you have established what you need in your garden you can dream about what you want with an eye on what is feasible.

It is necessary to explore your needs and wants at this stage of planning, even if you discover later that you got a bit carried away and your garden is just not big enough for everything you have on your lists. Now is also a good time to look at books and magazines for information. You need to consider what you can afford and, more urgently, what will grow in your soil, aspect and climate.

Wants Checklist

Wildlife pool	Summerhouse	Pergola
Arch	Trellis	Flat area for sports
Barbecue	Swimming pool	Bench/es
Fountain	Conservatory	Lighting
Irrigation	Fruit	Raised bed/s
Tree/Playhouse	Sandpit	Bridge
Arboretum		

12

A well planted pond can be a major feature in your garden.

ASPECT

Check the aspect of your garden.

Shady side: Only morning and evening sun in summer, often moist and cool.

East: Morning sun, perhaps cold drying winds.

Sunny side: Plants need extra watering.

West: Evening sun, perhaps rain, wind.

Note those areas of your garden which get the most sun and those which are in permanent shade and establish where the prevailing wind blows from, so that you don't have your sitting area in its path or plant any delicate flowers there. You might even find you have a wind tunnel in your garden, in which case a hedge, trellis or screen-block wall will deflect some of the wind without redirecting it at an increased speed as a solid wall would do.

SOIL

The soil provides your plants with food, water and support. Just dig a shallow hole and take a handful of soil out and feel it.

Sandy soil does not form crumbs, in fact it falls through your fingers. It is free draining but needs organic matter which will improve the structure so that it will retain food and water.

Clay soil is sticky and can become quite unworkable although it retains moisture and nutrients. This soil type needs cultivation. In autumn it should be dug or rotovated and left for the frost to break it down. In spring organic matter should be added again to lighten the structure and free the food and moisture.

Loam is a mixture of sand, clay and silt, the ideal soil to have in a garden. Working this soil makes gardening a pleasure. It is sticky enough to hold sufficient moisture, light enough to allow the excess water to drain away. This type of soil needs only the occasional addition of nutrients to make it the perfect growing medium for your plants.

Chalky soil is very light and provides little nourishment. It appears usually in a thin layer on porous chalk. Chalky soil is also alkaline; this of course limits the choice of plants that will grow on it. A regular addition of organic matter is absolutely essential to give your plants a chance.

The subsoil is a compact layer with little organic matter but it contains essential minerals. The surface of the subsoil should be broken up with a garden fork to aid the penetration of the roots which helps to support the plant. This is particularly important if you plant mature or semi-mature trees and shrubs.

You will be able to choose your plants in the confidence that they will grow well if you know the pH of your soil (this is a measure of the acidity or alkalinity of the soil). PH kits are available in garden shops and centres.

Sandy soil

Clay soil

Loam

Chalky soil

Neutral soil has a pH of 7; below 7 the soil is acidic and above 7 alkaline. There is a vast choice of plants which grow in a slightly acidic to slightly alkaline soil. Probably the best known plants which thrive on acidic soil are rhododendrons, camellias, heathers and pines but also vaccinium, pieris and zenobia and many more should be tried.

Again there are a vast number of plants which grow on chalky or alkaline soil, such as the Judas tree, yew, *Malus sieboldii*, *Rosa* 'Albéric Barbier' and verbascum. If your soil is alkaline and you want to grow rhododendrons and azaleas grow them in tubs. It is possible to change the pH of your soil. It is expensive and labour-intensive and this change will sometimes only last a season after which you will have to renew the soil.

When working in your garden avoid standing on the soil. It will damage the structure. A board laid on the ground will distribute your weight and limit the compression.

CLIMATE

It is useful to know your local climatic conditions. It will help you with the choice of your plants and avoid costly mistakes. Find out how high the rainfall is, what the temperatures are and how many hours of sunshine you can expect. The growing season starts later on top of a mountain than in a sheltered town garden. Record the sunny, shady, dry, wet, sheltered and exposed parts of your garden. It will then become obvious to you where to have your sitting area and you will be able to choose the right plants to suit your conditions. It is possible to alter the microclimate; trees, shrubs and fences make good shelter belts. The plants which are planted in these protected areas will benefit from the warmed up soil and flower and fruit all the more easily. Very sunny parts could be partially shaded by a specimen tree such as a flowering cherry or a *Gleditsia japonica*.

Prunus pendula 'Pendula Rosea', a fine weeping cherry.

15

Think of plants in combination, like these lupins and geraniums.

A shrub that is valuable for both its bright new leaves and beads of flowers, *Pieris formosa*.

HOW DO YOU ENJOY PLANTS?

Well ordered rows of pelargoniums and salvias or elegant drifts of lavender or exuberant muddles of poppies and peonies? There are no rules, but remember plants can enhance a good design or emphasize a bad one. They look best when grouped together against a strong framework of walls, hedges, paths and steps.

Most people who visit a garden centre buy a plant on impulse. It looks attractive and healthy and it makes a good show; it looked even better when it was part of the display. But where does this new plant fit into the existing planting scheme of your garden? More often than not it does not fit, it is the wrong colour, the wrong shape or needs special soil conditions. The plant is left standing around and eventually dies. A shopping list can prevent this sort of sad story.

Consider the following categories of plants for your garden:

Trees and Shrubs These may be shapely or shaped by you. They will be the most striking forms in the garden and will determine or emphasize the shape of the garden. A good number should be evergreen so that the shape does not fall away in winter.

Climbing Plants Do you have an ugly shed or bare wall you want to hide? Climbers can be trained over them, but additionally you can create a vertical garden with arches, trellises, pergolas, all festooned with plants blooming in sequence through the year.

Herbaceous Plants Amongst the framework of your architectural plants and structures for climbers you can plan the surge of flowers and foliage through the seasons and around your garden. You might want to highlight a particular season: the first bulbs of spring are always a cheerful token of the new year, for example, but try all the same to plan for a succession of effects so that each month brings a new and exciting event. A garden is not only about enjoying the present display but also about looking forward to the next.

Ground-cover Grass is the most common ground-cover; it is open, restful to the eye and you can sit on it, but you do need a minimum area for it to be useful. There are many shrubs and flowering plants that will cover ground that are attractive and will enhance the garden.

Roses and clematis make a classic combination of climbing plants. Here the rambler *Rosa* 'Albéric Barbier' is entwined with *Clematis* 'Polish Spirit'.

1. PREPARATION

Now is the time to consider what scope there is for your ideas.

LOOKING *at the* SITE

NOW THAT YOU HAVE MADE YOUR LISTS of needs and wants and have some idea what colours and types of plants you like, the time has come to take an inventory of your site. Draw a rough sketch of the outline of your garden and write on it what you discover. Record things like good view, poor view, which trees and plants you would like to keep, which areas of your garden are in the sun or shade at different times of the day and also at different times of the year. Do you have swampy areas or frost pockets? Find out the prevailing wind direction.

The lawn makes a restful central feature and the bench suggests that there is an interesting view. The path in the background indicates that the garden continues, adding mystery and inviting exploration.

◆ *The archway makes a suitable entrance to this peaceful part of the garden.*

Can your existing hard-landscape elements such as paths, terrace, pool, pergola, raised beds, retaining walls and steps be included in your new design? This fact-gathering exercise might be a little tedious at times but will make your design work later on so much easier.

Normally a herringbone pattern suggests a fast movement. Here the curves in the path slow the viewer down to enjoy the delightful border. It is important that curves are definite. They also act as a good foil to straight and solid boundaries.

One way of making a sloping garden interesting and easier to maintain is to introduce raised beds. Raised beds with imported soil allow plants to be grown which might otherwise not grow in the soil of the garden.

Steps are a very attractive feature in any garden. These easy steps, enhanced by the rose pergola, lead to a bench from which the garden can be seen in all its glory.

FLAT SITES

MAKING THE MOST OF YOUR SPACE is what good garden design is about. By now you will have become so familiar with your garden's aspect, its topography and the condition of the soil that ideas might begin to form in your mind. Here are some suggestions to help you to take advantage of apparent obstacles and learn to know what your limitations are.

To break up the horizontal line on a flat site introduce an area of paving. Planting architectural plants like phormiums or ferns alongside the paving would strengthen this idea.

An arch adds height to a flat garden. It can be smothered in roses, clematis and honeysuckle which delight the eye and will give fragrance for a long time. This arch divides the garden so that it cannot all be seen at one glance, which makes it much more interesting.

Flat sites need a strong ground pattern. The gravel paths with wooden edging and the geometric beds provide the perfect foil to the informal mounds of herbs.

◆ *The yellow, white and green colour scheme creates a convivial atmosphere in this parterre garden.*

YOU MIGHT NEED TO TERRACE a steep site. The retaining walls which hold up the terraces will give you a good opportunity to grow climbing or trailing plants. Fruit trees could be trained in attractive fans if the walls are sunny. A shady wall could be highlighted with a wall fountain or a succession of fountains surrounded by ivies, fatsia and hosta.

A steep site needs steps. Ideally the depth of the tread plus twice the height of the riser should add up to 66cm/26in.

A gentle slope could be made into a delightful rock garden using well weathered local stone. Plants grown here are (from the left) **snakeshead fritillary**, *Aubrieta* **'Blue Mist'** and **'Carnival'**, white *Saxifraga granulata* (fair maids of France), purple-pink *Saxifraga oppositifolia*, white *Saxifraga burseriana*, and a large clump of *Iberis sempervirens*.

23

GARDEN VIEWS

ALL GARDENS CAN HAVE VIEWS. Some views are borrowed, some can be framed, some have to be hidden and some invented. You might be able to open up a view into the countryside by removing a tree or part of a tall hedge. So look beyond your boundary to see if there is a pleasant area which you then can include visually in your garden.

Water is one of the most attractive focal points. The reflection varies with changing light and adds interest to the smallest garden.

This raised bed 'borrows' the trees outside the garden.

◆ *Note the different greens and texture of the foliage.*

The path is winding out of sight which invites exploration – it could be called a focal point in waiting.

◆ *Wisteria floribunda with its sunny foliage is a delightful climber even after flowering.*

THERE ARE TWO GOOD RULES on paving materials: use the best you can afford and don't use more than three different materials, otherwise you create too restless an atmosphere. Concrete pavers with either smooth or rough surfaces are not expensive and are widely available. Pebbles and stone or concrete flags make an interesting combination for paths.

Paving slabs of artificial stone in many size and colour variations are widely available and easy to lay.

Four of these patterned slabs form a circle which can create an interesting relief in an otherwise straight pattern.

The slabs act as stepping stones through a sea of gravel and plants. It is very attractive and yet not expensive.

Stone and cobbles are a pleasing combination of hard materials. The cobbles will provide better grip in wet weather.

This path is a sculpture enhanced by the irises in summer and, on its own, as a most valuable eye-catcher in winter.

◆ *The setts are laid proud of the gravel, thus containing it and making walking on this path easier.*

Granite setts are hard wearing and very attractive. Laying these setts will take longer but an infinite variety of interesting patterns can be created.

2. THE RULES

Many rules are made to be broken, but most are an invaluable help to the designer.

CONSIDER *the* WHOLE GARDEN

FIVE KEY PRINCIPLES

1. UNITY   Considering the house and garden as a whole.
2. SIMPLICITY   Fewer materials, features and colours make a visually effective garden.
3. SCALE and BALANCE   The proportions between the house and garden have to be 'right'.
4. HARMONY   Adjacent and opposite colours and their tints, tones and shades.
5. COMPOSITION   How all the elements in the garden fit together.

The brick path creates a break in this lusciously planted part of the garden. Without it the eye would not come to rest and the effect of the contrast in foliage texture and colour would be lost.

A modern interpretation of the cottage garden in quite a small area. The dense planting includes rodgersia, hemerocallis and the tall grass *Stipa gigantea* in flower.

◆ *A planting like this may seem simple and uncontrived, but you do in fact need to know your plants very well if you are to make it a success.*

A SENSE OF UNITY is best achieved if you design around one dominant idea. Everything else (beds, arch, water feature etc.) should be in scale to this idea but should play a secondary role. Climate or soil conditions can have a unifying effect on the garden. We associate pine trees and heathers with cool temperate gardens, palm trees and cacti with gardens in hot climates. With these groups of plants unity is achieved.

CONSIDER *the* WHOLE GARDEN

Unity has been achieved in this midsummer border of ornamental grasses. The clumps of pennisetum in the front catch the eye and lead on to the focal point, *Stipa gigantea*. Miscanthus and polystichum add to the flow.

This planting scheme of sun-loving plants is so successful because of the underlying strong symmetry of the house and path.

◆ *The borders are easy to maintain and there will always be something colourful to look at.*

KEEP IT SIMPLE

THE SMALLER THE GARDEN the more straightforward and uncluttered the design should be. If a feature does not add greatly to the design (e.g. a small rockery on the front lawn) leave it out. Simplicity of the ground pattern, planting and features, combined with a clear sense of purpose for every detail in your garden, will make it an enjoyable oasis.

This garden is a shady oasis. Moss is used as ground-cover and the stepping stones invite exploration. Stones and shrubs contrast well with the velvety surface of the moss. The bamboos and grasses form naturalistic screens which catch the light.

◆ *To keep this garden looking so attractive the moss has to be watered and weeded on a daily basis.*

Repetition of colour, texture or shape simplifies and unifies. The white of the foxgloves and the geraniums against their luscious green leaves are a perfect foil to the straight path and high walls.
'If it works, repeat it'. I don't know who made this observation first, but repetition does have a unifying and simplifying effect on the lay-out of your garden. Whether in the paving materials or the plant texture, grouping and colour it creates a flow between one part of the garden and another.

Simplicity, balance and harmony. This paved courtyard is almost maintenance free and a good solution where time is at a premium.

The simple, strong ground pattern of the paths in this garden set off the lavender (*Lavandula angustifolia*) beautifully. The low box square (*Buxus sempervirens*) is a suitable centre piece for the sitting area. It can be grown solid, like a table, or filled in with colourful or aromatic plants.

Everything *in* Balance

It is easy to recognize balance in a formal garden, for example where a central path is lined by hedges. Here the vertical space, the hedges, and the horizontal space, the path, should look as if they are in proportion around a central axis. Balance in an informal garden is not so easy to achieve where there is no obvious axis. But it is possible to create a similar sense of symmetry by balancing, for example, a circular pond in one part of the garden with a group of trees or a circular area of paving in another part.

The informality of a cottage garden, yet balance and order comes from the horizontal floorline of the tulips and herbaceous plants. The large shrubs help relate the garden to the house.

Perfect symmetry achieved by matching sets of hedges, clipped balls, spirals, terracotta pots and pillars. The focus in front is the central patterned circle on the ground.

A FOCAL POINT creates interest and gives your garden direction. In fact you can design the garden around a number of focal points, as long as you can see only one at a time. Otherwise you will lose the element of surprise and instead create a feeling of restlessness.

Scale in the garden is dictated by the house and its surroundings but most of all it has to relate to people. Even if your garden is very small, do not scale down the patio, path or steps, nor benches, arches or pergolas; all these elements have to be lifesize to be usable and comfortable. A helpful point to remember is, that the eye notices a mean dimension more easily than a generous one.

The axis of the paved path leads the eye to the single focus of a seat.

◆ *A pair of balanced but not identical borders softens the line.*

The vertical lantern and the horizontal line of the ground are linked by the mounded clipped shrubs.

Smaller terraces should be paved with smaller materials like bricks, setts or small paving slabs while the paving materials for large terraces can be stone flags or the larger slabs.

The depth of a paved sitting area adjacent to the house should ideally be half the height of the house wall at the eaves. If it is too narrow it will look stingy.

Trim borders of lavender either side of the basketweave path organize the view.

A calm central circle from which paths radiate is the stage for the sundial.

More informal but still balanced: cushions of santolina border the stone steps.

TRUE HARMONY

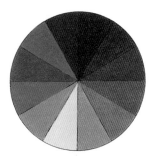

The colour wheel is a good aid. Colours which are adjacent to each other or opposite each other on the wheel look pleasing together.

The pale pastels of sisyrinchium, eschscholzia and osteospermum create a bed of subtle but lively tones.

◆ *Note how the mix of grey and green foliage suits this scheme.*

Shirley poppies and tree lupins are a delightfully frothy mixture, particularly effective in a single shade.

This is a very successful warm border, ranging through several colours of the spectrum. Their strength is accentuated by the strong greens of the leaves.

◆ *The paving strip at the edge allows plants to spill forward without impeding mowing.*

COLOURS CAN BE USED TO GREAT EFFECT. Blue with soft cream and soft yellow or soft pink with grey-green are serene colour combinations and usually look good in small gardens. The hazy effect of mauve, lilac, pale blue and pink creates depth; an excellent combination to have at the back of the garden. The bold colours, red, orange and bright yellow are foreground colours. To create greater depth in a bright border plant pale yellows or pale orange.

A delicate combination of pastel shades for a damp area of the garden – the pink *Astilbe* **'Venus'** against the glaucous leaves of *Hosta sieboldiana.*

COMPOSITION

IT IS QUITE AN ART to draw together all the components which make a garden. A garden should unfold gradually, contain enough interest (delightful plants, focal points, somewhere attractive to sit) and most of all should give pleasure. Great care should be taken not to destroy the composition by breaking what should be a coherent whole.

THE FUNCTIONAL ELEMENTS

Utilitarian features like dustbin, tool shed, oil tank, washing line or compost heap should be sited unobtrusively and yet be easily accessible. These functional features can be screened either by a hedge or divided off by an archway, pergola or trellis on which climbing plants can be trained. The paths leading to any of these features should be paved so that they can be used in all weathers.

This delicate planting scheme has been enlivened by self-sown orange poppies. They add a delightful spontaneity.

From this secret patio one can enjoy the last sunshine of the day. The planting is quite serene but comes alive in this light.

The sunken herb and vegetable garden has been laid out as a knot garden. The imaginative box hedged beds can be enjoyed even in winter.

A charming little formal paved and gravelled area which allows the eye to rest. From the luscious planting in the background we can assume that there are wonderful treats in store.

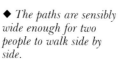

◆ *The paths are sensibly wide enough for two people to walk side by side.*

This path connects one sitting area with another. From the bench one can enjoy yet another part of the garden. Different areas relating to each other are the key to a successful garden.

Welsh poppies and aquilegia lightening up a shady part of the garden. The stone path blends in well with the informality of the planting scheme.

This summer show of bedding plants most certainly makes passers-by stop.

◆ *This type of planting is labour-intensive and expensive.*

The grasses and gravel are an ideal combination. The airy habit of the grasses makes them useful to hide visual barriers.

The simplicity of an area of well laid paving and lawn is very appealing. The planting enhances the architectural look.

This little summerhouse fits in well with the cottage garden planting and the stone steps.

The light and airy terrace is a good starting point from which to explore or view the garden.

◆ *The silvers, blues, pinks and white are a dynamic colour combination.*

3. THE DESIGN

Here are simple guidelines for drawing and implementing a plan.

SHAPES

SHAPES IN EXISTING GARDENS are seldom planned. A circular flower bed may become oval because more and more room for plants is needed. These evolved shapes can be charming but more often than not are uncertain in their outline. The eye constantly has to adjust the uncertain line to a shape which it recognizes. Look around – we are surrounded by shapes and patterns. Pre-existing shapes could be echoed or contrasted. The hexagonal shape of a bay window, for example, could become the shape of the lawn or that of the summerhouse. If you are surrounded by high buildings, you might like to contrast their shapes by introducing circles into your garden, a paved circle surrounded by round or dome shaped trees.

Geometrical shapes can quite often look severe when first laid out on the ground, but don't forget that any hard edges will be softened by plants.

SHAPES

Make the shapes in your garden deliberate. Interlocking circles, for example, are very pleasing. If the surface of one circle is grass and the other gravel edged with bricks, you create a sense of gentle movement. Asymmetrically arranged rectangles, some of them planted and some of them paved, create a similar effect. In fact the longer the shape, the faster the movement.

Paving material can influence the arrangement of shapes and movement in the garden. If you want to create a fast movement in your garden, pave the path with bricks laid in an herringbone pattern. A gravel or grass path slows down the movement. Here, tree trunks are like stepping stones and the curving path slows you to an amble.

DRAWING *a* PLAN

You will need a tape measure, pencil, scale rule, compass, set square and a large piece of graph paper. Pace the length and width of your garden (one pace measures roughly 1m/3ft), and select the scale which you want to use; 1:100 for a medium sized or 1:50 for a small garden.

It is important to remember the third dimension, height, particularly, if you include garden buildings (tool shed, summerhouse, pergola) in your design. Because of their height, the structures seem to foreshorten the horizontal areas and make the space between them appear smaller.

DESIGN IDEAS IN ONE'S HEAD can look quite unsuitable or out of proportion when implemented in isolation. For this reason you must draw an accurate plan of the whole garden. All the information about your garden should be recorded on this plan; from the position of the manholes to existing trees and shrubs which you would like to keep.

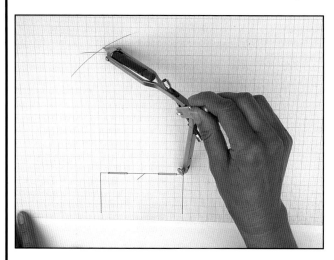

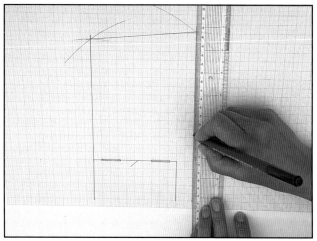

1. The best place to start surveying your garden is by measuring your house. It will become the base line from where to measure the perimeter of your garden. Draw the outline of your house on the graph paper marking the positions of windows and doors.
2. Take a measurement from one corner of the house to a corner of the boundary and record it.
3. Take the next measurement from the other corner of your house to the same corner of the boundary and record this as well.
4. Now plot these two measurements with the compass on the graph paper.
5. Continue creating these triangles from two known points to an unknown point right around the garden until you have recorded everything you need to know.
6. Join the plotted points and begin with the design work by laying a piece of tracing paper over the basic

plan. Draw the boundary free-hand on the tracing paper and start designing. Think of your terrace, paths and lawn first. These open areas, give your garden its shape. If you start with the flower beds first you will get into a frightful muddle.

7. Having decided on the shape of the clear areas, find the most sensible place for the functional features, then find a place for the features on your 'wants' list. Only now is the time to think about plants.

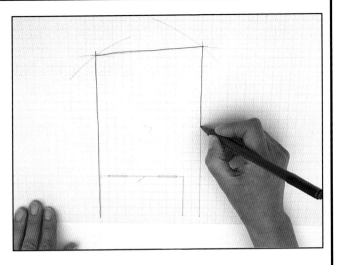

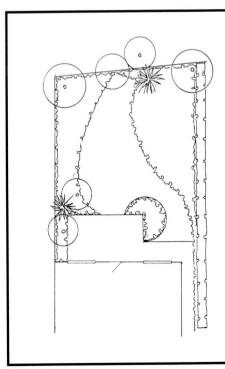

It will probably take several design attempts until you find one you are happy with. Take time over exploring and developing your ideas, even professional designers agonize sometimes for weeks before they are satisfied with the design. Here are two possibilities. One is a formal layout emphasizing the overall shape of the garden. The other is a terrace with an informal layout which tends to obscure the overall shape.

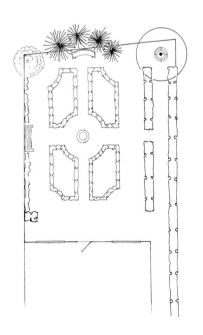

CREATING *from a* PLAN

WITH YOUR PLAN TO HAND, you should now be able to return to the garden and put it into effect. It is again a question of measuring accurately so that all the elements that make up your design fit in the positions assigned to them.

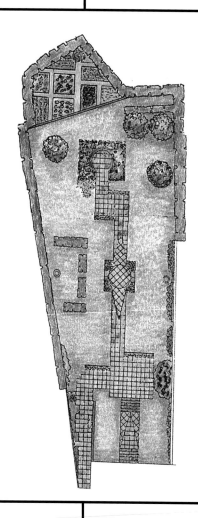

This is a plan to make the most of an irregularly shaped garden by laying a broad path with gazebos as a strong central feature. Opposite we show the important stages in laying the path from staking out the areas to the completion of construction.

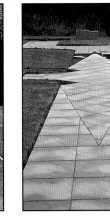

'Staking out' is vital for the success of any hard landscaping. String spanned between pegs gives an accurate outline.

◆ *It also helps you to assess that the planned paving has the right proportion for your garden.*

The strong, modern design of the path leads the eye on and will be a good contrast to the planting.

Descending steps into a garden gives you the feeling that you are entering a new space.

The completed path clearly gives the garden a new shape and image. When plants adorn the gazebos these will become a focus of interest and the staggered line of the path will draw the visitor down the garden. All the while the spaciousness and openness of the garden is preserved, perhaps even enhanced.

4. PLANTING THE GARDEN

This brief survey will give you an idea of the huge range of plants available and what can be done with them.

TREES *and* SHRUBS

PLANT TREES FIRST, not only because they take the longest to mature but they are also vitally important to the proportions of the planting scheme. Trees add structure to the garden, either as focal points within a border or as specimens planted in lawns or courtyards. Make sure you know the ultimate size of the tree: you might one day have to accommodate a monster.

This weeping *Malus*, crab-apple, makes a mushroom shape. 3 × 3m/10 × 10ft.

◆ *Crab-apples provide a wonderful selection of suitable subjects for the small garden.*

Although this cherry doesn't produce fruit, its flowering display is unequalled in spring. 9m/30ft

***Acer pseudoplatanus* 'Brilliantissimum'** A mop-head sycamore with shrimp-pink leaves in spring that turn gold then greenish. Slow to 4 × 4m/13 × 13 ft.

***Betula pendula* 'Youngii'** The dome of this weeping birch provides the opportunity for a shaded seat to be placed round its trunk. 3 × 3m/10 × 10ft

◆ *Train the leader up a stake to ensure a good shape.*

SHRUBS PROVIDE the next layer of planting. They are also structurally significant within the planting scheme. Many are good space dividers: even quite small shrubs can be planted to make a spatial division, indicating a change of style or mood.

The appearance of the same site (here, the foot of a warm wall) can be changed dramatically by different plantings. Above is a group consisting of the tree peony, *Paeonia suffruticosa*, *Choisya ternata* **'Aztec Pearl'** and *Hebe rakaiensis*. In the picture on the left, there is ***Cistus × cyprius***, **rosemary** and **lavender**, a choice of plants giving a Mediterranean effect. Note that both groups are predominantly evergreen so look good in winter.

CLIMBERS

CLIMBERS AND WALL SHRUBS are excellent space savers. Grown on trellises, fences, walls, poles, arches or pergolas they make a colourful screen, particularly if you plant several different climbers together.

Clematis viticella **'Royal Velours'** is a late-flowering variety, vigorous and easy. (Its host here is *Lavatera olbia rosea*.) 3m/10ft

Carpenteria californica Summer-flowering shrub. Needs a sheltering warm wall. ○, E, 1.5 × 1.5m/ 5 × 5ft

Rose 'American Pillar' A rambler with cottage associations which is vigorous, floriferous and easy. ○, 4.5m/15ft

Ceanothus 'Gloire de Versailles' Deciduous Californian lilac that blossoms in late summer. ○, E, 2.4 × 2m/8 × 6ft

Lonicera japonica **'Halliana'** Honeysuckle with scented flowers in summer and evergreen foliage. 4m/13ft

Camellia japonica **'Nobilissima'** Produces its beautiful double flowers very early in the year. ◑, E, 3 × 2m/10 × 6ft

Clematis chrysocoma Related to the montana clematis, but more refined and with good foliage. Spring-flowering. 6m/20ft

Euonymus fortunei **'Silver Queen'** A slow-growing shrub which is effective used as a climber. Lovely in a shady position. E, 2m/6ft

FLOWERS ARE THE HIGHLIGHTS of the garden and the third layer in the planting scheme, especially exciting grown against the framework of trees and shrubs. Ground-cover is the last layer and it draws the planting scheme together. Ground-cover plants are also good weed suppressors and prevent moisture from evaporating.

Tulip 'Spring Green' Bulbs are wonderful gap-fillers in beds. ○, 40 × 20cm/16 × 8in

Alstroemeria These tuberous perennials are not always easy to establish but very showy and good for cutting. Need shelter. ○, 60 × 30cm/2 × 1ft

Campanula punctata **'Rubriflora'** Tubular bells festoon this herbaceous plant in summer. 30 × 30cm/1 × 1ft

Salvia × superba **'May Night'** Herbaceous sage that blooms in mid to late summer. 45 × 45cm/ 1½ × 1½ft

Geranium sylvaticum **'Mayflower'** An easy, early-flowering geranium in almost any soil. 45 × 45cm/1½ × 1½ft

Phlox paniculata **'Little Lovely'** Phloxes are indispensable scented flowers of late summer. 60 × 60cm/2 × 2ft

Lamium maculatum A good ground-cover plant with silvery foliage and pink flowers in mid-spring. ◑, 15cm × 1m/ 6in × 3ft

◆ *There are also lamiums, or dead-nettles, with white flowers.*

BEDS *and* BORDERS

NOTHING IS MORE UPLIFTING than seeing a flower bed or border where the form, texture and colour of the plants have just the right balance of harmony and contrast. The arrangement of height is also important. Traditionally borders and beds have low plants with good foliage in the front such as those shown on this page.

Alchemilla mollis (Lady's mantle) Tiny golden star-flowers in summer but grown for its foliage. Self-sows invasively. 45 × 45cm/1½ × 1½ft

Helleborus argutifolius The Corsican hellebore produces its icy green flowers in early spring. E, 60 × 60cm/2 × 2ft

Stachys byzantina (Lamb's ears) Flowers in early summer. The non-flowering form is 'Silver Carpet.' 45 × 60cm/1½ × 2ft

***Heuchera* 'Palace Purple'** Flower-sprays in early summer. A distinctive perennial. 45 × 45cm/ 1½ × 1½ft

Bergenia cordifolia Valuable perennial for its early spring flowers and rounded leaves which may redden in winter. E, 45 × 45cm/ 1½ × 1½ft

***Geranium* 'Johnson's Blue'** is a most useful and beautiful mound-forming geranium. This very showy planting has the magenta *G. psilostemon* at the rear.

THE MIDDLE GROUND of the bed or border is usually reserved for flowers like peonies, phloxes, foxgloves, gladioli or perhaps a yucca for punctuation or small shrub for substance.

***Paeonia lactiflora* 'Emperor of India'** All the Imperial group of peonies are fabulously beautiful. Sun, good soil and peace is all they need. 1 × 1m/3 × 3ft

Eryngiums are some of the most architectural perennials with thistle heads in summer. O, 45cm to 2m/1½ to 6ft

***Aster* × *frikartii* 'Mönch'** is a fine aster, in bloom for months of the summer. Stake if necessary. O, 75 × 45cm/2½ × 1½ft

***Penstemon* 'Apple Blossom'** Bushy perennial flowering for a long period from midsummer. O, 45 × 45cm/1½ × 1½ft

Aquilegia Columbines are one of the joys of early summer. Wide colour range. Can be short-lived. 30 to 75cm/1 to 2½ft

Cistus* × *corbariensis One of the hardiest shrubby rock roses. O, E, 1 × 1m/ 3 × 3ft

◆ *Give this shrub a warm position and good drainage.*

53

BEDS *and* BORDERS

This bed has been planted with mostly white plants including polemonium and dicentra, but the blue geranium in the centre makes an effective foil. The striped grass in front is holcus.

***Paeonia suffruticosa* 'Sitifukujin'** A most glamorous Japanese tree peony with huge flowers. All these shrubs have handsome grey-green foliage. 1.2 × 1.2m/4 × 4ft

Hydrangea arborescens is a neat late-flowering mop-head which turns from white to green. Best in some shade. 1.4 × 1.4m/5 × 5ft

Rose 'Just Joey' A hybrid tea with large frilled and fragrant blooms and bronze-green foliage. Robust and upright in habit. 75 × 60cm/2½ × 2ft

***Hebe* 'Pewter Dome'** An excellent shrubby mound with glaucous leaves and white flowers in summer. O, E, 1× 1m/3 × 3ft

Lupins are cottage favourites with their peppery scented flowers in early summer. 75 × 75cm/ 2½ × 2½ft

Eremurus bungei The spires of all the foxtail lilies give height to a border. This one blooms in high summer. O, 1.4 × 45cm/5 × 1½ft

54

IN AN ISLAND BED, the taller plants are best saved for a central position. Here for example, the centre plant might well be a rose. However, in beds or borders backed by a fence or wall, tall plants tend to look best towards the rear. The stately spires of many perennials make excellent backdrops for a border, as can climbing plants grown into hedges, along walls or fences.

BEDS *and* BORDERS

A perfect pastel combination for summer of mauve delphiniums in front of the old shrub rose 'Fantin Latour'.

× *Fatshedera lizei* A cross between fatsia and ivy, this sprawling evergreen shrub is often used as a climber. Give support. ●, 2m/6ft

Cardoon (*Cynara cardunculus*) backs tulip 'Queen of Night' and *Tellima grandiflora*.

◆ *Black and grey make a dramatic and moody combination.*

SEASONS *of* INTEREST

WINTER

Evergreens come into their own in winter but deciduous trees and shrubs also make the garden interesting. The shape of the individual plant is much more noticeable now and it will be apparent if it adds to or detracts from the overall design. The garden can also look colourful with winter flowers and the bright-barked branches and trunks of cornus and birch.

Hamamelis mollis, the Chinese witch hazel, underplanted here with snowdrops and aconites (*Eranthis*).

Narcissus lobularis is a small species daffodil, a form of the Lent lily. Here its blooms are unspoilt by snow. 20cm/3in

Helleborus orientalis 'Ellen Terry' A beautiful form of the Lenten hellebore, easy evergreen perennials for shade. 30 × 45cm/1 × 1½ft

SPRING
Bulbs are probably the most prominent plants in spring. The choice becomes wider and wider. Trees and shrubs are bursting into flower and the fresh green of their leaves transforms the garden into a glowing stage.

Primula vulgaris **'Sibthorpii'** A mauve form of the common primrose which grows well on heavy soil. ☽, 7.5 × 15cm/3 × 6in

Fritillaria meleagris The snakeshead fritillary has chequered bells though a white form of this bulb is also common. 20cm/8cm

Erythronium **'White Beauty'** A tuberous plant which forms good clumps. ☽, 20 × 10cm/8 × 4in

Crocus tommasinianus A rapidly spreading and self-seeding little crocus. 10cm/4in

Pulsatilla vulgaris The Pasque flower is beautiful even after flowering with its large silky seedheads. O, 15 × 30cm/6in × 1ft

Magnolia stellata The star magnolia makes a small spreading shrub, producing its flowers on bare branches. 2 × 2m/6 × 6ft

Chionodoxa luciliae The Glory-of-the-snow is an early-spring flowering bulb. Will naturalize well in grass. 10cm/4in

Pieris japonica **'Mountain Fire'** A shrub with brilliant new foliage, and strings of pearly flowers. Acid soil. ☽, E, 3 × 3m/10 × 10ft

Tulip **'China Pink'** A reliable healthy 'lily-flowered' tulip, named after its elegant waisted shape. O, 45cm/1½ft

SEASONS *of* INTEREST

Roses are the most seductive shrubs. This group of old roses, Gallicas, are very scented and beautiful but only once-flowering.

SUMMER

As the sun gets hotter, so do the colours. This is the time when perennials and annuals are at their best, and shrubs and trees seem to retreat into the background. But there are some stunning performers which need mentioning.

Cistus **'Elma'** A fine rock rose with very large blooms. Fairly hardy but still needs good drainage and shelter. O, E, 2 × 1.2m/6 × 4ft

Primula pulverulenta The candelabra primulas are elegant perennials for a moist position in semi-shade. 45 × 30cm/1½ × 1ft

Violas are wonderful subjects for tucking into the front of beds, often weaving their way through taller plants. 15 × 20cm/6 × 8in

Polemonium **'Lambrook Mauve'** Flowers in early summer and recurrently for the rest of the season. 45 × 30cm/1½ × 1ft

Veronica gentianoides Easy perennial for any soil. Ice blue flowers in early spring. 45 × 45cm/ 1½ × 1½ft

◆ *The photograph shows an unusual form called 'Tissington White'*

Osteospermum jucundum A hardy form of the African daisy which folds its petals towards the evening. O, 30 × 30cm/1 × 1ft

AUTUMN

There is an interesting juxtaposition of misty light and fiery colours in autumn, of mauve asters and scarlet maples. The yellows and reds of acers, rudbeckias, and helianthus build up to a crescendo before the trees lose their leaves.

Nerine bowdenii Beautiful bulb flowering in late autumn. Protect in winter or lift and re-plant in spring. ○, 45cm/18in

***Cotoneaster salicifolius* 'Exburyensis'** A robust fast-glower with masses of yellow berries that follow its tiny white flowers. E, 5 × 5m/16 × 16ft

◆ *This arching shrub demands plenty of space.*

Helianthus Perennial sunflowers are a brilliant addition to the late border. ○, 1.2 to 2.2m/4 to 7ft

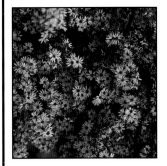

***Aster cordifolius* 'Sweet Lavender'** A bushy tall aster with sprays of flowers. It should be staked. ○, 1.2 × 1m/4 × 3ft

***Sedum* 'Autumn Joy'** Handsome perennial with cool green then russet flower heads, and glaucous leaves. 60 × 60cm/2 × 2ft

Acer The maples are indispensable shrubs and trees for fiery leaf colour in autumn.

◆ *Make sure you buy a good named variety. Seedling trees don't always colour well.*

PLANT ASSOCIATIONS

A spring picture which combines the domed shape of the shrub skimmia, with the green sword leaves of iris.

◆ Spiraea *'Arguta' gives an airy background to these strong shapes.*

A wonderfully fresh spring border composed of contrasting blues and yellows: *Kerria japonica* is the dominant shrub with forget-me-nots around.

◆ *Bowles' golden grass (*Milium effusum *'Aureum') to the left self-sows lightly.*

Forget-me-nots (***Myosotis***) form a cool haze around the fiery red of *Euphorbia griffithii* 'Fireglow'.

Another simpler wilder variant of blue and yellow: bluebells (*Hyacinthoides*) and Welsh poppies (*Meconopsis cambrica*).

Some plants make a dramatic impact by themselves, but most are more effective in a planned combination. The convergence of colour and foliage can be breathtaking. It is also great fun to place plants together to create magnificent pictures.

A pastel mix of foliage and flowers: *Symphytum × uplandicum* 'Variegatum', honesty (*Lunaria*), and forget-me-nots.

Artistic pinks in spring: a viridiflora tulip and the poker heads of the bistort, *Polygonum (Persicaria) bistorta* 'Superbum'.

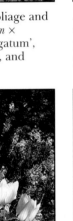

The white of the tulip 'Purissima' is reinforced by white honesty with cream/green foliage.

Harmonies: the lime heads of *Euphorbia characias* surround the tulips 'Spring Green' and 'Fringed Elegance'.

A classic partnership: tulip 'China Pink' in a sea of forget-me-nots (*Myosotis*).

◆ *This is one of the most popular of all spring bedding combinations.*

61

PLANT ASSOCIATIONS

The round globes of peony and saucer flowers of the white rose are given vertical interest from *Sisyrinchium striatum*.

A gentle combination of light and dark pinks is achieved by this mingling of centaurea and aquilegias.

The purple *Geranium himalayense* 'Gravetye' is lit up by the pale pink *G. endressii*.

These lilies and eryngium (sea holly) make beautiful and practical partners as the latter acts as a stake, propping the lily up.

Glowing colour in semi-shade: tall yellow ligularias in the rear, Bowles' golden sedge (*Carex elata* 'Aurea') to the right, yellow *Primula florindae* and burnt orange mimulus spilling over in front.

◆ *All these plants thrive in a moist position.*

Clever contrasts in shape and colour: purple geraniums make mounds below the tall spires of yellow asphodels.

The little blue viola forms a carpet around the white mallow, *Malva moschata alba*, both in flower for a long period.

Warm yellows and blue-mauves in high summer with anthemis and salvias.

A successful combination of a small shrub and a perennial: French lavender (*Lavandula stoechas*) grows behind *Polygonum* (*Persicaria*) *bistorta* 'Superbum'.

A haze of blue Love-in-a-mist (*Nigella*) makes a contrast to the strong uprights of the burgundy *Gladiolus byzantinus* in this densely planted border.

◆ *The display will be continued through the summer with delphiniums and ornamental onions.*

FOLIAGE EFFECTS

FOLIAGE PLANTS will give a luxuriant appearance to the garden, whether in sun or shade. Many of the larger ones are dramatic enough to be given a key position by themselves, whilst others are most effective when partnered with plants that have contrasting leaves. Some have the bonus of good flowers too.

Caragana arborescens **'Lorbergii'** is an arching shrub with yellow pea flowers and grassy leaves. 2.4 × 1.5m/8 × 5ft

A border of bronze, silver, grey and green foliage. The dark fennels give a misty effect.

All maples have graceful foliage. This example, *Acer palmatum* 'Dissectum Viride' has very finely cut leaves and forms a dome of 1.3m/4ft high and wide.

◆ *Grow in semi-shade as the delicate leaves can scorch in sun.*

At the damp base of a wall, ferns, hostas and *Darmera peltata*, the umbrella plant, are well placed.

Ivy is useful as a backdrop or to cover an eyesore. This variegated form of *Hedera helix* is good in semi-shade. E.

This hosta is in full flower, but it is the shapely leaves which we notice from late spring until autumn.

FOLIAGE EFFECTS

A good contrast is made between the grassy leaves of the golden sedge and the rounded foliage of the witch hazel (*Hamamelis*).

Bergenia purpurascens leaves turn beetroot in winter. It has red flowers in spring. E, 45 × 30cm/ 1½ × 1ft

The leaves of purple cotinus and silvery eucalyptus enhance each other, spiced with the blue of veronica beneath.

Silver-leaved *Artemisia ludoviciana* is a perfect foil to the pink flowers of Japanese anemones.

◆ *Always consider silver leaves in your planting schemes.*

Trillium grandiflorum roseum. Needs a moist, well-drained soil. ●, 40 × 30cm/1ft 4in × 1ft

◆ *It also requires neutral to acid soil.*

Rhododendrons cannot tolerate lime. Give them humus-rich acid soil and plant them in semi-shade. E

***Epimedium × youngianum* 'Niveum'** A perennial with spring flowers which needs moist but well-drained soil. ◑, 30 × 30cm/1 × 1ft

Halesia monticola The snowdrop tree needs sun and a moist, well-drained soil. 6 × 4m/20 × 13ft

◆ *It thrives better in neutral to acid earth.*

***Ceanothus* 'Trewithen Blue'** A vigorous spring-flowering shrub which needs wall shelter. ◐, E, 6 × 6m/20 × 20ft

Helianthemum All rock roses need full sun and a well-drained soil. E, 15 × 45cm/6in × 1½ft

PLANTS HAVE THEIR OWN REQUIREMENTS. Some insist on sun or shade, others on a moist or well-drained soil, and a number require an acid soil. These needs have to be met if the plants are to thrive.

This group of plants is admirable for a sheltered position in full sun. The silvery *Elaeagnus angustifolia* (Oleaster) is the perfect foil for the dark leaves of the evergreen *Carpenteria californica*, summer-blooming. At their feet is *Phlomis fruticosa* (the Jerusalem sage). All require well-drained soil though the carpenteria will not succeed in a droughty position.

5. EXAMPLE GARDENS

Four very different open spaces and how they were made into gardens.

A TOWN GARDEN

A NEWLY CONVERTED MEWS was going to be used for offices, and off road car parking was a requirement for which gravel was specified. The yard has very high stone and brick walls.

REQUIREMENTS

– Paving near the offices
– Water feature
– Sitting area
– Pergola
– Colourful narrow
  borders

The paving near the house is Portland stone which reflects the reddish tint of the stone walls. The water feature is in three parts. The water cascades out of a cast iron spout into a stone trough and then into the pond. All walls are smothered in climbers and provide interest all year.

The border shows the subtle colour scheme, with roses 'Iceberg', 'Fantin Latour' and 'Blairii Number Two'.

◆ *The roses are trained along wires which are almost invisible.*

The pebbles around the pond are a good contrast to the stone paving. The clumps of hostas and hemerocallis seem to float.

Humulus lupulus 'Aureus', *Clematis montana*, *Wisteria sinensis* and *Clematis* 'Jackmanii' cover this pergola.

Rose 'Constance Spry' is a vigorous, healthy rose with a fine scent and looks good even on a brick wall.

Roses 'Constance Spry' and 'Heritage' have been underplanted with *Philadelphus* 'Manteau d'Hermine' and *Thymus × citriodorus* 'Aureus'.

◆ *Both roses flower for a long time and can be grown as bushy shrubs.*

This charming bench is at the highest point in the garden. The view from here is breathtaking.

The view from the bench towards the house.

View from the terrace towards the *sitting area*. The path is lined with old roses which are underplanted with *Stachys byzantina*.

◆ *Old roses flower only once but they are beautiful and require little maintenance.*

Climbing roses and *Hydrangea anomala* ssp. *petiolaris* underplanted with lavender and pinks in front of the house.

THIS GARDEN is right on top of a hill, in a very exposed position with splendid views. The existing mature hedge along the southern boundary has a herbaceous and shrub border in front of it and a large terrace providing a sitting area.

A COTTAGE GARDEN

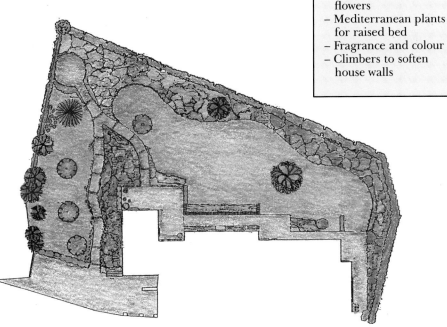

The outline of the lawn is very definite and adds crispness to the picture. It is more interesting if there is a range of greens and foliage shapes in planted areas.

Now in its third year the garden looks very established. The outline of the lawn detracts from the straight high hedge, introduces movement and increases the depth of the garden. Once the hedges have grown around the terrace it will be a very cosy place to enjoy the garden even in winter.

A
Medium-
sized
Garden

THIS GARDEN consisted mainly of a flat lawn with borders along the edge. I introduced circles to give the garden greater depth and create a contrast with the squareness of the house. The tranquillity of the front garden can be enjoyed in the evening sun.

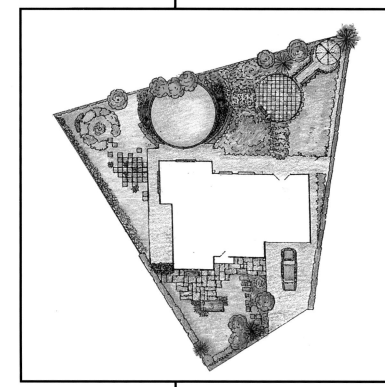

My main aim for this garden was to distract the eye from the boundary. The circles achieve this. The planting along the fence blends in well with the mature trees beyond the fence. The garden appears much larger. The patio on the side is for pots with plants of winter interest which can be enjoyed from inside the house. The front garden is functional and yet has the atmosphere of a garden.

A MEDIUM-SIZED GARDEN

The view from the grass circle to the paved circle. The planned pergola over the gravel path will add the intended mystery.

The paving stones are set below the turf surface to make mowing easier. The old pear tree is an ideal climbing frame for the rose.

The blossoms of the cordon apples will form an attractive screen in spring and a productive one in autumn.

The fence behind the rose garden is smothered in Rose 'Rambling Rector'. It will also grow well over arches.

Shrubs and herbaceous plants will soften and add height to the strong design of paving, paths and lawn circle.

◆ *The brick edges of the circles and paths harmonize with the brickwork of the house.*

Rose 'Coral Satin' grows on the west wall of the house. The delightful coral-pink flowers glow in the evening light.

A LARGE GARDEN

REQUIREMENTS

– Extend terrace
– Steps for interest
– Raised flower beds
– Disguise fence
– Shed
– Fruit trees
– Colour
– Easy maintenance

THIS GARDEN WAS LAID TO GRASS by the builders with one existing silver birch tree – a truly green field site. A narrow area of paving along the length of the house was used as the sitting area. The high close boarded fence formed the boundary.

The slightly upward sloping ground allowed me to outline the extended terrace with a brick wall and a step. The design for the main part of the garden is a series of interlocking circles and fragments of circles. I wanted to divide the garden into separate areas of interest and needs without creating any harsh boundaries.

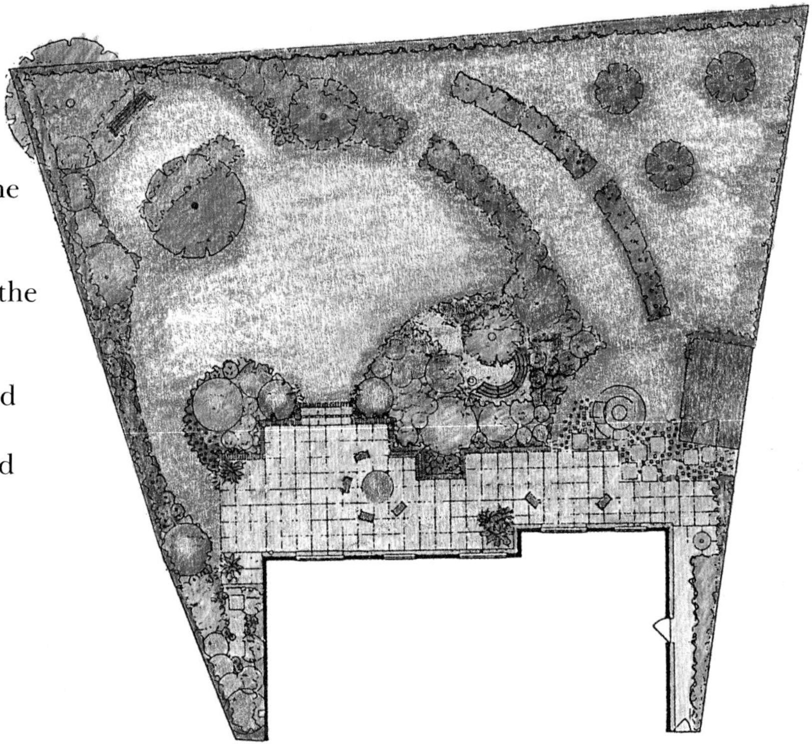

The circular sitting area will soon be completely hidden from the rest of the garden.

A view along the new terrace and brick wall. The planting will soften the outline in time.

This lovely bench is not only an attractive feature but also comfortable. It soon will have sweet smelling climbers growing behind it.

The strong ground pattern of the garden can be enjoyed particularly from above (these pictures were taken from upstairs in the house). The hedges will create a green division which will invite exploration.